TAKING CHARGE

WHAT TO DO IF YOUR IDENTITY IS STOLEN

I0426296

Contact info is provided on the inside back cover.

INTRODUCTION

Identity theft happens when someone steals your personal information and uses it without your permission. It is a serious crime that can wreak havoc with your finances, credit history, and reputation – and it can take time, money, and patience to resolve. The Federal Trade Commission (FTC), the nation's consumer protection agency, prepared this guide to help you repair the damage that identity theft can cause, and reduce the risk of identity theft happening to you.

If you suspect that someone has stolen your identity, acting quickly is the best way to limit the damage. Setting things straight involves some work. This guide has tips, worksheets, blank forms, and sample letters to guide you through the recovery process. It covers:

- what identity theft victims must do immediately

- what problems may crop up

- how you can reduce your risk of identity theft

How do thieves get my information?

"I thought I kept my personal information to myself."

You may have, but identity thieves are resourceful and use a variety of ways to get your information. They "dumpster dive" or rummage through your garbage, the trash of businesses, or public dumps. They may work – or pretend to work – for legitimate companies, medical offices, clinics, pharmacies, or government agencies, and take advantage of that role to convince you to reveal personal information. Some thieves pretend to represent an institution you trust, and try to trick you by email (phishing) or phone (pretexting) into revealing personal information.

What do identity thieves do with my information?

Once identity thieves have your personal information, they can drain your bank account, run up charges on your credit cards, open new utility accounts, or get medical treatment on your health insurance. An identity thief might even file a tax return in your name and get your refund. In some extreme cases, a thief might even give your name to the police during an arrest.

How can I tell that someone has stolen my information?

- you see unexplained withdrawals from your bank account

- you don't get your bills or other mail

- merchants refuse your checks

- debt collectors call you about debts that aren't yours

- you find unfamiliar accounts or charges on your credit report

- medical providers bill you for services you didn't use

- your health plan rejects your legitimate medical claim because the records show you've reached your benefits limit

- the Internal Revenue Service (IRS) notifies you that more than 1 tax return was filed in your name, or that you have income from an employer you don't work for

- you get notice that your information was compromised by a data breach at a company where you do business or have an account

- you are arrested for a crime someone else allegedly committed in your name

What should I do if my information is lost or stolen, but my accounts don't show any problems?

If your wallet, Social Security card, or other personal, financial, or account information is lost or stolen, contact the credit reporting companies and place a fraud alert on your credit file. See how to place a fraud alert on page 6. Check your bank and other account statements for unusual activity. You may want to take additional steps, depending on what information was lost or stolen. For example, you can exercise your legal right to a free copy of your credit report.

If your information is lost in a data breach, the organization that lost your information will notify you and tell you about your rights. Generally, you may choose to:

- place a fraud alert on your credit file

- monitor your accounts for unusual activity

- exercise your right to a free copy of your credit report

You may have other rights under state law.

IMMEDIATE STEPS

This section explains the first steps to take if your identity is stolen:

1. Place an Initial Fraud Alert
2. Order Your Credit Reports
3. Create an Identity Theft Report

MONITOR YOUR PROGRESS

As you get started, create a system to organize your papers and track deadlines.

ITEM	HOW TO TRACK	TIPS
Telephone Calls	Create a log of all telephone calls.	• Record the date of each call and the names and telephone numbers of everyone you contact. • Prepare your questions before you call. Write down the answers.
Postal Mail	Send letters by certified mail. Ask for a return receipt.	• See sample letters starting at page 43.
Documents	Create a filing system.	• Keep all originals. • Send copies of your documents and reports, not originals. Make copies of your identification to include in letters.
Deadlines	Make a timeline.	List important dates, including when: • You must file requests • A company must respond to you • You must send follow-up

1 Place an Initial Fraud Alert

Three nationwide credit reporting companies keep records of your credit history. If you think someone has misused your personal or financial information, call 1 of the companies and ask them to put an initial fraud alert on your credit report. You must provide proof of your identity. The company you call must tell the other companies about your alert.

An initial fraud alert can make it harder for an identity thief to open more accounts in your name. When you have an alert on your report, a business must verify your identity before it issues credit in your name, so it may try to contact you. Be sure the credit reporting companies have your current contact information so they can get in touch with you. The initial alert stays on your report for 90 days. It allows you to order 1 free copy of your credit report from each of the 3 credit reporting companies.

HOW TO PLACE A FRAUD ALERT

STEP BY STEP:	NOTES:		
☐ Contact 1 credit reporting company.	**Equifax** *1-800-525-6285*	**Experian** *1-888-397-3742*	**TransUnion** *1-800-680-7289*
	☐ Report that you are an identity theft victim. ☐ Ask the company to put a fraud alert on your credit file. ☐ Confirm that the company you call will contact the other 2 companies.		
	Placing a fraud alert is free. The initial fraud alert stays on your credit report for 90 days.		
	Be sure the credit reporting companies have your current contact information so they can get in touch with you.		
☐ Learn about your rights.	*The credit reporting company will explain that you can get a free credit report, and other rights you have.*		
☐ Mark your calendar.	*The initial fraud alert stays on your report for 90 days. You can renew it after 90 days.*		
☐ Update your files.	☐ Record the dates you made calls or sent letters. ☐ Keep copies of letters in your files.		

You may want to contact the credit reporting companies to place a credit freeze on your credit file. A credit freeze means potential creditors cannot get your credit report. That makes it less likely an identity thief can open new accounts in your name. The cost to place and lift a freeze depends on state law. In many states, identity theft victims can place a freeze for free, but in others, victims must pay a fee, which is usually about $10. If you have a police report, you may be able to place or lift a freeze for free.

Putting a credit freeze on your credit file does not affect your credit score. If you place a credit freeze on your credit file, you can:

- get a copy of your free annual credit report

- open a new account, apply for a job, rent an apartment, buy insurance, refinance your mortgage, or do anything else that requires your credit report

If you want a business, lender, or employer to be able to review your credit report, you must ask the credit reporting company to lift the freeze. You can ask to lift the freeze temporarily or permanently. You may be charged a fee to lift the freeze.

HOW TO REQUEST A CREDIT FREEZE

STEP BY STEP:	NOTES:		
☐ Contact your state Attorney General's office.	*Find your state Attorney General's office at www.naag.org to determine what your state allows.*		
	☐ Ask if there is a fee for putting a freeze on your credit file. ☐ Ask how long the freeze lasts.		
☐ Contact **each** credit reporting company.	*Equifax* *1-800-525-6285*	*Experian* *1-888-397-3742*	*TransUnion* *1-800-680-7289*
	☐ Report that you are an identity theft victim. ☐ Ask the company to put a freeze on your credit file. ☐ Pay the fee required by state law.		
☐ Mark your calendar.	*Your state law determines how long the credit freeze lasts.*		
☐ Update your files.	☐ Record the dates you made calls or sent letters. ☐ Keep copies of letters in your files.		

2 Order Your Credit Reports

After you place an initial fraud alert, the credit reporting company will explain your rights and how you can get a copy of your credit report. **Placing an initial fraud alert entitles you to a free credit report from each of the 3 credit reporting companies.**

HOW TO ORDER YOUR FREE CREDIT REPORTS

STEP BY STEP:	NOTES:		
☐ Contact **each** credit reporting company.	*Equifax* *1-800-525-6285*	*Experian* *1-888-397-3742*	*TransUnion* *1-800-680-7289*
	☐ Explain that you placed an initial fraud alert. ☐ Order your free copy of your credit report. ☐ Ask each company to show only the last 4 digits of your Social Security number on your report.		
☐ Update your files.	☐ Record the dates you made calls or sent letters. ☐ Keep copies of letters in your files.		

Contact Businesses

If you know which of your accounts have been tampered with, contact the related businesses. Talk to someone in the fraud department, and follow up in writing. Send your letters by certified mail; ask for a return receipt. That creates a record of your communications.

When you read your credit report, you may find unauthorized charges or accounts. Learn how to review your credit report and dispute errors on page 13.

③ Create an Identity Theft Report

An Identity Theft Report helps you deal with credit reporting companies, debt collectors, and businesses that opened accounts in your name. You can use the Report to:

- get fraudulent information removed from your credit report

- stop a company from collecting debts that result from identity theft, or from selling the debt to another company for collection

- place an extended fraud alert on your credit report

- get information from companies about accounts the identity thief opened or misused

Creating an Identity Theft Report Involves 3 Steps:

1. Submit a complaint about the theft to the FTC. When you finish writing all the details, print a copy of the report. It will print as an Identity Theft Affidavit.

2. File a police report about the identity theft, and get a copy of the police report or the report number. Bring your FTC Identity Theft Affidavit when you file a police report.

3. Attach your FTC Identity Theft Affidavit to your police report to make an Identity Theft Report.

Some companies want more information than the Identity Theft Report includes, or want different information. The information you need to provide depends on the policies of the credit reporting company and the business that sent the information about you to the credit reporting company.

HOW TO REPORT IDENTITY THEFT TO THE FTC AND PRINT AN FTC IDENTITY THEFT AFFIDAVIT

ONLINE

STEP BY STEP:	NOTES:
☐ Complete the FTC's online complaint form.	*www.ftc.gov/complaint* ☐ Complete the complaint form with as many details as you know. ☐ Review the form and click "submit." ☐ Save the complaint reference number that appears after you submit your information. *You'll need your complaint reference number to update your complaint online or by phone.*
☐ Save or print your FTC Identity Theft Affidavit.	☐ Click on the words "Click here to get your completed FTC Identity Theft Affidavit." *Before you leave that screen, be sure you saved or printed your Affidavit. You cannot save or print it after you leave this screen.*

OR

BY PHONE

STEP BY STEP:	NOTES:
☐ Call the FTC.	*1-877-438-4338* *1-866-653-4261 (TTY)* ☐ Tell the representative what happened. ☐ Ask for your complaint reference number and Affidavit password. *The FTC representative will email you a link so you can get your Affidavit.*
☐ Save or print your FTC Identity Theft Affidavit.	☐ Go to the link the representative sent you. ☐ Enter your complaint reference number, Affidavit password, and your email address. ☐ Print or save your Identity Theft Affidavit.

THEN

STEP BY STEP:	NOTES:
☐ Update your files.	☐ Record the dates you filed your complaint. ☐ Keep copies of your Affidavit in your files.
☐ If necessary, call the FTC to update your complaint.	*1-877-438-4338* *1-866-653-4261 (TTY)* *Be ready to provide your complaint reference number.*

HOW TO FILE A POLICE REPORT

STEP BY STEP:	NOTES:
☐ Go to your local police department or the police department where the theft occurred.	☐ Bring a copy of your FTC Identity Theft Affidavit and any other proof of the theft. ☐ Complete a report about the theft. ☐ Ask to have a copy, or the number, of the report. *In some states, police must take your report. Visit www.naag.org to see what your state law requires.* *If the police won't take a report about the identity theft, ask if you can file a "miscellaneous incidents" report, or go to a different police station, or the sheriff's department, state police or federal authority.* *You can give police a copy of the FTC's Memo to Law Enforcement, which explains how Identity Theft Reports are important to victims. See the memo in the back of this book on page D-1.*
☐ Update your files.	☐ Record the dates you made calls or visits. ☐ Record your police report number. ☐ Keep a copy of your police report in your files.

HOW TO CREATE YOUR IDENTITY THEFT REPORT

STEP BY STEP:	NOTES:
☐ Attach your FTC Identity Theft Affidavit to your police report.	☐ Keep a complete copy in your files.

If you are a victim of identity theft and have created an Identity Theft Report, you can place an extended fraud alert on your credit file. It stays in effect for 7 years. When you place an extended alert:

- you can get 2 free credit reports within 12 months from each of the 3 nationwide credit reporting companies

- the credit reporting companies must take your name off marketing lists for prescreened credit offers for 5 years, unless you ask them to put your name back on the list

HOW TO PLACE AN EXTENDED FRAUD ALERT

STEP BY STEP:	NOTES:
☐ Contact **each** credit reporting company. *See contact info on inside back cover.*	☐ Ask the company to place an extended fraud alert on your credit file. *The company may have you complete a request form.* ☐ Include a copy of your Identity Theft Report when you submit the form and your letter. *Placing an extended fraud alert is free.*
☐ Mark your calendar.	*The extended alert stays in effect for 7 years.*
☐ Update your files.	☐ Record the dates you made calls or sent letters. ☐ Keep copies of letters in your files.

Review Your Credit Reports

If you know an identity thief tampered with some of your accounts, you may have contacted the related businesses already. After you get your credit reports, read them to see whether other fraudulent transactions or accounts are listed.

Your credit report is full of information about where you live, how you pay your bills, and whether you've been sued or arrested, or have filed for bankruptcy. The information in your credit report is used to evaluate your applications for credit, insurance, employment, and renting a home, so it's important that the information is accurate and up-to-date. Check all key information, including your:

- name
- address
- Social Security number
- employers

If you see errors on the report, like accounts you didn't open or debts you didn't incur, contact the credit reporting companies and the fraud department of each business that reported an error.

Dispute Errors with Credit Reporting Companies

If you find mistakes when you review your credit reports, send letters explaining the mistakes to:

- the 3 nationwide credit reporting companies
- the fraud department of each business that reported a fraudulent transaction on your existing accounts
- the fraud department of each business that reported a new account opened in your name by an identity thief

If the errors result from identity theft and you have an Identity Theft Report, ask the credit reporting companies and business to block the disputed information from appearing on your credit reports. The credit reporting companies must block transactions and accounts if you are an identity theft victim. Read about blocking on page 17.

HOW TO DISPUTE ERRORS WITH CREDIT REPORTING COMPANIES

STEP BY STEP:	NOTES:
☐ Write to each credit reporting company. *See contact info on inside back cover.* *See sample letter on page C-1.*	☐ Explain that you are an identity theft victim. ☐ List the errors that you found. ☐ Include copies of documents showing the errors. ☐ Ask the credit reporting company to remove fraudulent information. *The credit reporting company must investigate the items you send, and forward that information to the business that reported the information to the credit reporting company.*
☐ Receive response from each credit reporting company.	*If your credit file changes because of the business' investigation, the credit reporting company must send you a letter with the results.* *If the credit reporting company puts the information back in your file, it must send you a letter telling what it did.*
☐ Update your files.	☐ Record the dates you made calls or sent letters. ☐ Keep copies of letters in your files.

After the business gets notice from the credit reporting company, it has 30 days to investigate and respond to the credit reporting company. If the business finds an error, it must notify the credit reporting company so your credit file can be corrected. If your credit file changes because of the business' investigation, the credit reporting company must send you a letter with the results. The credit reporting company can't add the disputed information back into your file unless the business says the information is correct. If the credit reporting company puts the information back in your file, it must send you a letter telling you that.

HOW TO DISPUTE FRAUDULENT CHARGES ON YOUR EXISTING ACCOUNTS

STEP BY STEP:	NOTES:
☐ Change the passwords or PINs for your accounts.	*See tips on creating a strong password on page 42.*
☐ Ask each business if it will accept your Identity Theft Report or if it uses special dispute forms.	☐ If you must use the business' forms, ask for blank forms.
☐ Write to the fraud department of each business.	☐ Use the address they specify for disputes. ☐ Explain that you are an identity theft victim. ☐ List the errors you found. ☐ Send copies of documents that show the error. ☐ Ask the business to remove fraudulent information. ☐ Include a copy of your Identity Theft Report (or the special dispute forms if the business requires them). ☐ Include a copy of your credit report. Black out any personal information that does not pertain to your dispute. *See sample letter at the back of this book on page A-1.* *The business must review your letter, investigate your complaint, and tell you the results of their investigation. If the information is wrong, the business must tell the credit reporting company.*
☐ Ask the business to send you a letter confirming that it removed the fraudulent information.	☐ Keep the letter in case you see fraudulent information on your statement later.
☐ Update your files.	☐ Record the dates that you changed passwords and PINs. ☐ Record the dates you made calls or sent letters. ☐ Keep copies of letters in your files.

HOW TO DISPUTE FRAUDULENT ACCOUNTS OPENED IN YOUR NAME

STEP BY STEP:	NOTES:
☐ Contact the fraud department of each business where an account was opened.	☐ Explain that you are an identity theft victim. ☐ Close the account. ☐ Ask if the business will accept your Identity Theft Report or if it uses special dispute forms. If you must use the business' forms, ask for blank forms.

☐ Send a copy of your Identity Theft Report or the business' dispute forms.	*See sample letter at the back of this book on page B-1.*
	
	☐ Ask the business to send you a letter confirming that:
	   • the fraudulent account isn't yours
	   • you aren't liable for it
	   • it was removed from your credit report
	
	☐ Keep the letter and use it if you see this account on your credit report in the future.

☐ Update your files.	☐ Record the dates you made calls or sent letters. ☐ Keep copies of letters in your files.

Blocking: Report Errors to the Credit Reporting Companies

By law, credit reporting companies must block identity theft-related information from appearing on a victim's credit report. They must block unauthorized transactions, accounts, and inquiries. To get unauthorized information blocked, you must give information to the credit reporting companies.

HOW TO ASK CREDIT REPORTING COMPANIES TO BLOCK INFORMATION

STEP BY STEP:	NOTES:
☐ Write to each credit reporting company. *See contact info on inside back cover.*	☐ Send a copy of your Identity Theft Report. ☐ Include proof of your identity including your name, address, and Social Security number. ☐ Explain which information on your report resulted from identity theft and that the information didn't come from a transaction you made or approved. ☐ Ask the company to block the fraudulent information. *You can get sample letters at www.ftc.gov/idtheft.*
☐ Update your files.	☐ Record the dates you made calls or sent letters. ☐ Keep copies of letters in your files.

If the credit reporting company accepts your Identity Theft Report, it must block the fraudulent information from your credit report within 4 business days after accepting your Report, and tell the business that sent the fraudulent information about the block.

If the credit reporting company rejects your Identity Theft Report, it can take 5 days to ask you for more proof of the identity theft. It has 15 more days to work with you to get the information, and 5 days to review information you sent. It may reject any information you send after 15 days. It must tell you if it won't block information. You can re-submit the Report.

After a business has been notified about a block of fraudulent information, it must:

- stop reporting that information to all the credit reporting companies.

- not sell or transfer a debt for collection.

Blocking: Report Errors to Businesses

Contact the business that sent the inaccurate information that appears on your credit report. Send a copy of your Identity Theft Report and a letter explaining what is inaccurate. After the business gets your Report, it must stop reporting the inaccurate information to the 3 nationwide credit reporting companies. However, the business still can try to collect a debt, and sell or transfer the debt to a collection company.

To prevent a business from collecting, selling or transferring a debt to a collection agency, you must contact the credit reporting companies and ask them to block fraudulent information. To do this, follow the steps on page 17, How to Ask Credit Reporting Companies to Block Information.

HOW TO ASK A BUSINESS TO BLOCK INFORMATION

STEP BY STEP:	NOTES:
☐ Write to the business that has records of the fraudulent transactions.	☐ Include a copy of your Identity Theft Report. ☐ Include proof of your identity, including your name, address, and Social Security number. ☐ Include a copy of your credit report. ☐ Explain which information on the credit report resulted from identity theft, and that it didn't come from a transaction you made or approved. *The business must stop reporting the inaccurate information to the 3 nationwide credit reporting companies. The business can continue to try to collect the debt, and sell or transfer the debt to a collection company.* *To prevent a business from collecting, selling or transferring a debt, follow the steps on page 17.* *You can get sample letters at www.ftc.gov/idtheft.*
☐ Update your files.	☐ Record the dates you made calls or sent letters. ☐ Keep copies of letters in your files.

Get Copies of Documents the Identity Thief Used

Ask for copies of any documents the identity thief used to open a new account or make charges in your name. These documents can help prove the identity theft.

HOW TO GET COPIES OF DOCUMENTS THE IDENTITY THIEF USED

STEP BY STEP:	NOTES:
☐ Contact the business that has records of transactions the identity thief made. OR	☐ Ask for copies of documents the thief used to open new accounts or charge purchases in your name. ☐ Send details about where or when the fraudulent transactions took place. ☐ Include a copy of your Identity Theft Report or the proof the business requires, and proof of your identity.
☐ Give written permission to a law enforcement officer to contact the company on your behalf.	*The business must send you free copies of the records within 30 days of getting your request. For example, if you dispute a debt on a credit card account you did not open, ask for a copy of the application and applicant's signature.* *You can get sample letters at www.ftc.gov/idtheft.*
☐ Update your files.	☐ Record the dates you made calls or sent letters. ☐ Keep copies of letters in your files.

ATM and Debit Cards

As an identity theft victim, you have protections under federal law for ATM or debit card transactions. Federal law also limits your liability for the unauthorized electronic transfer of funds that result from identity theft.

It's best to act as soon as you discover a withdrawal or purchase you didn't make or authorize. Many card issuers have voluntarily agreed that an account holder will not owe more than $50 for transactions made with a lost or stolen ATM or debit card. However, under the law, the amount you can lose depends on **how quickly** you report the loss. If you don't report within 60 days of the day your institution sent you the account statement showing the unauthorized withdrawals, you could lose all the money an identity thief took from your account.

HOW TO REPORT FRAUDULENT TRANSACTIONS

STEP BY STEP:	NOTES:
☐ Contact your ATM or debit card issuer.	☐ Report the fraudulent transaction. *Act as soon as you discover a withdrawal or purchase you didn't make.*
☐ Write a follow up letter to confirm that you reported the problem.	☐ Keep a copy of your letter. ☐ Send it by certified mail and ask for a return receipt.
☐ Update your files.	☐ Record the dates you made calls or sent letters. ☐ Keep copies of letters in your files.

Limit Your Loss

HOW QUICKLY YOU REPORT THE PROBLEM *after your card issuer sends you the statement showing unauthorized purchases or withdrawals*	YOUR MAXIMUM LOSS
Within 2 business days	$50
2-60 business days later	$500
More than 60 business days later	All the money taken from your ATM/debit card

In most cases, the financial institution has 10 business days to investigate your report of a fraudulent transaction. It must tell you the results within 3 days of finishing the investigation and fix an error within 1 business day of finding it. In some cases, it can take 45 days to finish the investigation.

Checking Accounts

An identity thief may steal your paper checks, misuse the account number from the bottom of your checks, or open a new account in your name. If this happens, contact your bank or financial institution and ask them to close the account as soon as possible.

Federal law doesn't limit your loss if a thief forges your signature on your checks or uses your account number to buy something by phone, but most states hold banks responsible for losses from those fraudulent transactions. However, banks expect their customers to take reasonable care of their accounts. That means you might be responsible for a loss if you know about a problem but don't report it to your bank quickly.

HOW TO REPORT STOLEN CHECKS

STEP BY STEP:	NOTES:
☐ Contact your financial institution.	☐ Ask it to stop payment on stolen checks and close your account. ☐ Ask it to report the theft to its check verification system. *The check verification system will tell businesses to refuse the stolen checks.*
☐ Update your files.	☐ Record the dates you made calls or sent letters. ☐ Keep copies of letters in your files.

OR

STEP BY STEP:	NOTES:
☐ Contact check verification companies.	☐ Report that your checks were stolen. ☐ Ask them to tell businesses to refuse the stolen checks. *TeleCheck* *Certegy, Inc.* *1-800-710-9898* *1-800-437-5120*
☐ Update your files.	☐ Record the dates you made calls or sent letters. ☐ Keep copies of letters in your files.

HOW TO REPORT CHECKING ACCOUNTS OPENED IN YOUR NAME

STEP BY STEP:	NOTES:
☐ Contact ChexSystems, Inc., to request a free ChexSystems report.	☐ Order a free copy of the ChexSystems report that lists checking accounts opened in your name. **ChexSystems, Inc.** *www.consumerdebit.com* *1-800-428-9623*
☐ Contact every financial institution where a new account was opened.	☐ Ask the financial institution to close the account.
☐ Update your files.	☐ Record the dates you made calls or sent letters. ☐ Keep copies of letters in your files.

WHAT IF A BUSINESS REJECTS YOUR CHECK?

STEP BY STEP:	NOTES:
☐ Ask the business for an explanation.	*The business must tell you what information it used to decide to reject the check.*
☐ Update your files.	☐ Record the dates you made calls or sent letters. ☐ Keep copies of letters in your files.

WHAT IF A THIEF PASSES BAD CHECKS IN YOUR NAME?

STEP BY STEP:	NOTES:
☐ Contact the business that took the bad check.	☐ Explain that you are a victim of identity theft before they start collection action against you.
☐ Update your files.	☐ Record the dates you made calls or sent letters. ☐ Keep copies of letters in your files.

If you are working with a bank or financial institution to resolve identity theft-related problems and need help, contact the agency that oversees the bank or financial institution.

Visit www.ffiec.gov/consumercenter to find out which agency to contact.

Credit Cards

Your liability for credit card charges that you didn't authorize is limited to $50 per card. To dispute fraudulent charges, contact the credit card issuer within 60 days of the day the credit card issuer sends you the bill showing the fraudulent charges.

What if an identity thief changed the address on your account and you don't get your statement? You are responsible for keeping track of your statements. If your statement doesn't arrive on time, contact your credit card company.

HOW TO DISPUTE FRAUDULENT CHARGES ON YOUR CREDIT CARD

STEP BY STEP:	NOTES:
☐ Write to your credit card issuer.	☐ Write within 60 days of the day the credit card issuer sent you the bill showing the fraudulent charges. ☐ Write to the address specified for billing inquiries, not the payment address. ☐ Identify the amount and date of the billing error. ☐ Include your name, address, account number, and a copy of your Identity Theft Report or other proof of identity theft. ☐ Send the letter by certified mail and ask for a return receipt. *See sample letter at the back of this book on page A-1.* *Within 30 days of getting your complaint, the credit card company must send you a letter acknowledging it, unless your complaint has been resolved. The company must resolve the dispute within 2 billing cycles, or in less than 90 days after getting your complaint.*
☐ Update your files.	☐ Record the dates you made calls or sent letters. ☐ Keep copies of letters in your files.

Bankruptcy Filed in Your Name

If you believe someone filed for bankruptcy in your name, contact the U.S. Trustee in the region where the bankruptcy was filed. The U.S. Trustee Program refers cases of suspected bankruptcy fraud to the United States Attorneys for possible investigation and prosecution. The U.S. Trustee can't provide you with legal help, so you may need to hire an attorney.

HOW TO REPORT BANKRUPTCY FILED IN YOUR NAME

STEP BY STEP:	NOTES:
☐ Write to the U.S. Trustee in the region where the bankruptcy was filed.	☐ Find regional offices at www.usdoj.gov/ust or in the Blue Pages of the phone book under U.S. Government Bankruptcy Administration. ☐ Describe the situation and provide proof of your identity.
☐ Consider hiring an attorney.	*An attorney can explain to the court that the bankruptcy filing was fraudulent.*
☐ Update your files.	☐ Record the dates you made calls or sent letters. ☐ Keep copies of letters in your files.

Investment Accounts

If an identity thief has tampered with your investments or brokerage accounts, contact your broker, account manager, and the U.S. Securities and Exchange Commission (SEC).

HOW TO DEAL WITH AFFECTED INVESTMENT ACCOUNTS

STEP BY STEP:	NOTES:
☐ Call your broker or account manager.	☐ Describe the situation.
☐ File a complaint with the SEC.	*www.sec.gov/complaint.shtml* or write to: *SEC Office of Investor Education and Advocacy* *100 F Street, NE* *Washington, DC 20549*
☐ Call the SEC for general information.	*1-800-732-0330*
☐ Update your files.	☐ Record the dates you made calls or sent letters. ☐ Keep copies of letters in your files.

Debt Collectors

A debt collector may contact you if an identity thief opens accounts in your name but doesn't pay the bills. To stop contact and collection action, contact the debt collector, the business that opened the fraudulent account, and the credit reporting companies.

HOW TO DISPUTE A DEBT WITH A DEBT COLLECTOR

STEP BY STEP:	NOTES:
☐ Write to the debt collector within 30 days after you get written notice of the debt.	☐ Tell the debt collector you are a victim of identity theft and don't owe the debt. ☐ Send copies of your police report, Identity Theft Report, or other documents that detail the identity theft. *The collector must suspend collection efforts until it sends you written verification of the debt. If the collector works for another company, it must tell the other company you are an identity theft victim.* *See How to Permanently Stop Calls and Letters from a Debt Collector on page 26.*
☐ Contact the business where the fraudulent account was opened.	☐ Explain that this is not your debt. ☐ Ask for information about the transactions that created the debt. *The business must give you details about the transaction if you ask. For example, if you dispute a debt on a credit card account you did not open, ask for a copy of the application and applicant's signature.*
☐ Contact the 3 nationwide credit reporting companies.	☐ Take steps to have fraudulent information blocked from your credit report and to stop a business from selling or transferring a debt for collection. *Follow the steps on page 17, How to Ask Credit Reporting Companies to Block Information.*
☐ Update your files.	☐ Record the dates you made calls or sent letters. ☐ Keep copies of letters in your files.

HOW TO STOP A DEBT COLLECTOR FROM SELLING OR TRANSFERRING A DEBT

Follow the steps on page 17, How to Ask Credit Reporting Companies to Block Information.

After each credit reporting company accepts your Identity Theft Report, it must tell the debt collector that the debt may be caused by identity theft. Then, the debt collector can't sell or transfer the debt or report it to a credit reporting company.

HOW TO PERMANENTLY STOP CALLS AND LETTERS FROM A DEBT COLLECTOR

STEP BY STEP:	NOTES:
☐ Write a letter to the debt collector.	☐ Tell them to stop contacting you about the debt.
	After the debt collector gets the letter, it can't contact you again, except once – to say it won't contact you again, or that it plans to take specific action. Sending this letter should stop calls and letters from the collector, but it doesn't prevent the debt collector from suing you to collect the debt.
	To stop collection action, follow the steps on page 17.
	You can get sample letters at www.ftc.gov/idtheft.
☐ Update your files.	☐ Record the dates you made calls or sent letters.
	☐ Keep copies of letters in your files.

Government-Issued Identification

If your government-issued identification – for example your driver's license, passport, or Medicare card – has been lost, stolen, or fraudulently misused, contact the agency that issued the identification.

HOW TO REPORT A LOST, STOLEN OR MISSING DRIVER'S LICENSE

STEP BY STEP:	NOTES:
☐ Contact the Department of Motor Vehicles in your state.	☐ Cancel the lost or stolen item and get a replacement.
	☐ Ask the agency to put a note in your file so no one else can get a license or ID in your name.
☐ Update your files.	☐ Record the dates you made calls or sent letters.
	☐ Keep copies of letters in your files.

HOW TO REPORT A LOST, STOLEN OR MISSING PASSPORT

STEP BY STEP:	NOTES:
☐ Contact the U.S. Department of State.	www.travel.state.gov/passport
	OR
	Find a local Department of State office online or in the Blue Pages of the phone book.
☐ Update your files.	☐ Record the dates you made calls or sent letters.
	☐ Keep copies of letters in your files.

Mail Theft

Sometimes an identity thief steals mail and uses it to get your personal and financial information, open new accounts, or commit tax fraud. The U.S. Postal Inspection Service, which investigates cases of identity theft, wants you to contact them and make a report.

HOW TO REPORT MAIL THEFT

STEP BY STEP:	NOTES:
☐ Contact the U.S. Postal Inspection Service office near your home.	*Find the nearest office at https://postalinspectors.uspis.gov* **OR** *Go to your local post office to find the address.*
☐ Update your files.	☐ Record the dates you made calls or sent letters. ☐ Keep copies of letters in your files.

Utilities

An identity thief may use your personal and financial information to get telephone, cable, electric, water, or other services. Report fraudulent accounts to the service provider as soon as you discover them.

HOW TO REPORT FRAUDULENT UTILITY CHARGES AND ACCOUNTS

STEP BY STEP:	NOTES:
☐ Contact the utility or service provider.	☐ Close the account that the identity thief opened.
☐ Contact your state Public Utility Commission for additional help.	*Search online at www.naruc.org/commissions or check the Blue Pages of your phone book.*
☐ Contact the Federal Communications Commission for help with cell phone or telephone services.	*1-888-225-5322* *1-888-835-5322 (TTY)* *Consumer & Governmental Affairs Bureau* *445 12th Street, SW* *Washington, DC 20554* *www.fcc.gov/cgb*
☐ Update your files.	☐ Record the dates you made calls or sent letters. ☐ Keep copies of letters in your files.

Student Loans

An identity thief may use your personal or financial information to get a student loan. Contact the school or program that opened the loan and ask them to close the loan.

HOW TO REPORT FRAUDULENT STUDENT LOANS

STEP BY STEP:	NOTES:
☐ Contact the U.S. Department of Education.	www.ed.gov/about/offices/list/oig/hotline.html 1-800-647-8733 U.S. Department of Education Office of the Inspector General 400 Maryland Avenue, SW Washington, DC 20202
☐ Update your files.	☐ Record the dates you made calls or sent letters. ☐ Keep copies of letters in your files.

Misuse of Social Security Number

An identity thief may steal your Social Security number and sell it, or use the number to get a job or other benefits. Contact the Social Security Administration when you discover any misuse of your Social Security number.

HOW TO REPORT MISUSE OF YOUR SOCIAL SECURITY NUMBER

STEP BY STEP:	NOTES:
☐ Contact the Social Security Administration.	www.socialsecurity.gov Fraud Hotline 1-800-269-0271 1-866-501-2101 (TTY) Social Security Administration Fraud Hotline P.O. Box 17785 Baltimore, MD 21235
☐ Update your files.	☐ Record the dates you made calls or sent letters. ☐ Keep copies of letters in your files.

Income Taxes

If someone uses your Social Security number to get a job, the employer will report the person's earnings to the Internal Revenue Service (IRS). When you file your tax return, you won't include those earnings. But, IRS records will show you failed to report all your income, and you can expect to get a letter from the IRS.

If someone uses your Social Security number and files a tax return in your name before you file, they may get your refund. When you file your own return later, IRS records will show the first filing and refund, and you'll get a letter from the IRS.

If you think someone has misused your Social Security number to get a job or tax refund – or the IRS sends you a notice indicating a problem – contact the IRS immediately. Specialists will work with you to protect your account.

HOW TO REPORT INCOME TAX FRAUD

STEP BY STEP:	NOTES:
☐ Contact the Internal Revenue Service.	*IRS Identity Protection Specialized Unit* *1-800-908-4490* *www.irs.gov/identitytheft* ☐ Report the fraud and ask for the IRS ID Theft Affidavit Form 14039. ☐ Send a copy of your police report or an IRS Identity Theft Affidavit Form 14039 and proof of your identity, such as a copy of your Social Security card, driver's license or passport.
☐ Update your files.	☐ Record the dates you made calls or sent letters. ☐ Keep copies of letters in your files.

Medical Identity Theft

If an identity thief gets medical treatment using your name, the thief's medical information – for example, blood type, test results, allergies, or illnesses – can get into your medical file. Information about the thief can be added to your medical, health insurance, and payment records.

If you suspect an identity thief has used your medical information, get copies of your medical records. Under federal law, you have a right to know what's in your medical files. Contact each doctor, clinic, hospital, pharmacy, laboratory, health plan, and anywhere you believe the thief has used your information. For example, if a thief got a prescription in your name, ask for the record from the pharmacy that filled the prescription and the health care provider who wrote the prescription. You may need to pay a fee to get copies of your records.

A provider might refuse to give you copies of your medical or billing records because it thinks that would violate the identity thief's privacy rights. A provider who thinks that is mistaken: you have the right to know what's in your file. If a provider denies your request, you have a right to appeal. Contact the person the provider lists in its Notice of Privacy Practices, the patient representative, or the ombudsman. Explain the situation and ask for your file. If the provider refuses to provide your records within 30 days of your written request, you may complain to the U.S. Department of Health and Human Services' Office for Civil Rights at www.hhs.gov/ocr.

The medical provider or office that created the information must change any inaccurate or incomplete information in your files. They also should tell labs, other health care providers, and anyone else that might have gotten incorrect information. If an investigation doesn't resolve your dispute, ask that a statement of the dispute be included in your record.

If a debt collector contacts you about a medical bill incurred by an identity thief, read more about dealing with debt collectors on page 25.

HOW TO CORRECT ERRORS IN YOUR MEDICAL RECORDS

STEP BY STEP:	NOTES:
☐ Contact each health care provider and ask for copies of your medical records.	☐ Check your state's health privacy laws. Some state laws make it easier to get copies of your medical records. *Visit www.hpi.georgetown.edu/privacy/records.html to review your state law rights.* ☐ Complete the request form and pay any fees required to get copies of your records. *If your provider refuses to give you copies of your records because it thinks that would violate the identity thief's privacy rights, you can appeal. Contact the person the provider lists in its Notice of Privacy Practices, the patient representative, or the ombudsman. Explain the situation and ask for your file.* *If the provider refuses to provide your records within 30 days of your written request, you may complain to the U.S. Department of Health and Human Services Office for Civil Rights at www.hhs.gov/ocr.*
☐ Review your medical records and report any errors to your health care provider.	☐ Write to your health care provider to report mistakes in your medical records. ☐ Include a copy of the medical record showing the mistake. ☐ Explain why this is a mistake and how to correct it. ☐ Include a copy of your police report or Identity Theft Report. ☐ Send the letter by certified mail and ask for a return receipt. *Your health care provider should respond to your letter within 30 days. It must fix the mistake and notify other health care providers who may have the same mistake in their records.*
☐ Notify your health insurer and all 3 credit reporting companies.	☐ Send copies of your police report or Identity Theft Report to your health insurer's fraud department and the 3 nationwide credit reporting companies. *See contact info on inside back cover.*
☐ Order copies of your credit reports if you haven't already.	*See page 8. Check to see if there are debts caused by an identity thief.*
☐ Consider placing a fraud alert or security freeze on your credit files.	*See page 6.*
☐ Update your files.	☐ Record the dates you made calls or sent letters. ☐ Keep copies of letters in your files.

Child Identity Theft

Child identity theft happens when someone uses a child's personal information to commit fraud. A thief may steal and use a child's information to get a job, government benefits, medical care, utilities, car loans, or even a mortgage. Avoiding, discovering, and recovering from child identity theft involves some unique challenges.

Parents and guardians don't expect a minor child to have a credit file and rarely request or review their child's credit report. A thief who steals a child's information may use it for many years before the crime is discovered. The victim may learn about the theft years later, when applying for a job, loan, or apartment, or when a business reviews the credit file and finds fraudulent accounts.

A parent or guardian can check whether a minor child has a credit report if they think the child's information is at risk, say if the child's Social Security card was lost, a school or business leaked the child's personal information to the public, or bill collectors or government agencies contact the child about accounts the child didn't open. To get a minor child's credit report, a parent or guardian must contact the credit reporting companies and provide proof of identity and other documents.

HOW TO FIND OUT IF A CHILD HAS A CREDIT REPORT

STEP BY STEP:	NOTES:
☐ Contact each of the 3 nationwide credit reporting companies.	*Email TransUnion: childidtheft@transunion.com.* *Call Experian (1-888-397-3742) and Equifax (1-800-525-6285).* ☐ Ask for a manual search of the child's file. *The companies will check for files relating to the child's name and Social Security number, and for files related only to the child's Social Security number.* *The credit reporting companies may require copies of:* • *the child's birth certificate listing parents* • *the child's Social Security card* • *the parent or guardian's government-issued identification card, like a driver's license or military identification, or copies of documents proving the adult is the child's legal guardian* • *proof of address, like a utility bill, or credit card or insurance statement*
☐ Update your files.	☐ Record the dates you made calls or sent letters. ☐ Keep copies of letters in your files.

If you find out that someone has misused your child's personal information, follow these steps:

HOW TO HELP A CHILD VICTIM OF IDENTITY THEFT

STEP BY STEP:	NOTES:
☐ Contact each of the 3 nationwide credit reporting companies.	☐ Send a letter asking the companies to remove all accounts, inquires and collection notices associated with the child's name or personal information. ☐ Explain that the child is a minor and include a copy of the Uniform Minor's Status Declaration. *See form in the back of this book on page I-1.*
☐ Place a fraud alert.	*See how to place a fraud alert on page 6.*
☐ Learn about your rights.	*The credit reporting company will explain that you can get a free credit report, and other rights you have.*
☐ Consider requesting a credit freeze.	*See how to request a credit freeze on page 7.* *The credit reporting companies may ask for proof of the child's and parent's identity.*
☐ Order the child's credit report.	*See how to order your free credit reports on page 8.*
☐ Contact businesses where the child's information was misused.	*See how to contact businesses on page 8.*
☐ Create an Identity Theft Report.	*See how to create an Identity Theft Report on page 9.*
☐ Read Next Steps.	*See next steps on page 13.*
☐ Update your files.	☐ Record the dates you made calls or sent letters. ☐ Keep copies of letters in your files.

Criminal Violations

If an identity thief uses your name, date of birth, Social Security number, or other personal information during an investigation or arrest, the information will be added to your state's criminal database. The information also may be added to a national criminal database.

If you learn who the thief is, ask the criminal records database manager(s) to change the "key name" in the database. That way, the records will show the thief's name instead of yours. Contact the agency that made the arrest, the court that convicted the identity thief, and your state Attorney General's office to get documents that will help you show your innocence.

HOW TO CLEAR YOUR NAME OF CRIMINAL CHARGES

STEP BY STEP:	NOTES:

☐ Contact the law enforcement agency that arrested the thief.	☐ File a report about the impersonation.
	☐ Give copies of your fingerprints, photograph, and identifying documents.
	☐ Ask the law enforcement agency to:
	  • compare your information to the imposter's
	  • change all records from your name to the imposter's name
	  • give you a "clearance letter" or "certificate of release" to declare your innocence

☐ Keep the clearance letter or "certificate of release" with you at all times.	
☐ Update your files.	☐ Record the dates you made calls or sent letters. ☐ Keep copies of letters in your files.

WHAT TO DO IF A COURT PROSECUTED A CASE AGAINST A THIEF WHO USED YOUR NAME

STEP BY STEP:	NOTES:
☐ Contact the court where the arrest or conviction happened.	☐ Ask the district attorney for records to help you clear your name in court records. ☐ Provide proof of your identity. ☐ Ask the court for a "certificate of clearance" that declares you are innocent.
☐ Keep the "certificate of clearance" with you at all times.	
☐ Contact your state Attorney General.	*Find your state Attorney General's office at www.naag.org.* ☐ Ask if your state has an "identity theft passport" or some kind of special help for identity theft victims.
☐ If you obtain an identity theft passport, keep it with you at all times.	
☐ Consider hiring a criminal defense lawyer.	*Your state Bar Association or Legal Services provider can help you find a lawyer. See contact info on inside back cover.*
☐ Contact information brokers.	*Information brokers buy criminal records and create criminal records files to sell to employers and debt collectors.* ☐ Ask the law enforcement agency that arrested the thief for the names of information brokers who buy their records. ☐ Write to the brokers and ask them to remove errors from your file.
☐ Update your files.	☐ Record the dates you made calls or sent letters. ☐ Keep copies of letters in your files.

REDUCE YOUR RISK

Review Your Credit Reports

You have the right to get a free copy of your credit report every 12 months from each of the 3 nationwide credit reporting companies. Your credit report may show the first signs that someone has misused your information, so it's important to check your report a few times a year. Ordering 1 free report every 4 months lets you monitor your file and spot errors early.

You can get your free credit report at www.annualcreditreport.com or by calling 1-877-322-8228. You must give your name, address, Social Security number, date of birth, and the answers to questions that only you would know – for example, "How much is your monthly mortgage payment?" Each credit reporting company may ask you for different information. Use the form in the back of this book (page G1) to request your annual credit report by mail. For more information, visit www.ftc.gov/idtheft.

You also are entitled to a free copy of your credit report if:

- a company takes an adverse action against you, like denying your application for credit, insurance, or employment. You must ask for your report within 60 days of receiving notice of the adverse action. The notice will give you the name, address, and phone number of the credit reporting company to contact.

- you are unemployed and plan to look for a job within 60 days

- you are on public assistance

- your report is inaccurate because of fraud, including identity theft

Otherwise, a credit reporting company may charge you a fee for an additional copy of your report within a 12-month period. To buy a copy of your report, contact:

Equifax	Experian	TransUnion
1-800-685-1111	1-888-397-3742	1-800-916-8800
www.equifax.com	www.experian.com	www.transunion.com

Read Your Account and Billing Statements

- Look for charges you didn't make.

- Be alert for bills that don't arrive when you expect them.

- Follow up if you get credit card or account statements you don't expect.

Correct any errors as soon as possible.

Review Your Explanation of Medical Benefits

Call your medical insurer and health care provider if you see items that surprise you in your Explanation of Medical Benefits.

Respond Quickly to Notices from the Internal Revenue Service

If you get a notice from the IRS that suggests someone misused your Social Security number, respond quickly to the address included with the notice. The notice may say that you didn't pay taxes on a job you know you never held, or that your Social Security number was used on another return. Remember that the IRS never makes first contact with taxpayers by email, and doesn't ask for personal information through email. If you get email that claims to be from the IRS, call the IRS before you respond. Call 1-800-829-1040 for more information.

If you find out that an identity thief has used your Social Security number on a tax return, call the IRS's Specialized Identity Theft Protection Unit at 1-800-908-4490.

Identity Theft Protection Services

Should you pay a company to monitor your financial accounts, credit reports, and personal information? Many people find it valuable and convenient to pay a company for monitoring services. Other people choose to exercise their legal rights and protect their information for free. When you understand your rights, it can be easier to decide if you want to use a commercial service.

Before you buy an identity theft protection or monitoring product or service, get the details. Know exactly what you're paying for, as well as the total cost of the service.

Active Duty Alerts for Military Personnel

Military personnel have additional protections. If you're deployed, you can place an active duty alert on your credit reports to help minimize the risk of identity theft while you're away. Active duty alerts last for 1 year. If your deployment lasts longer, renew the alert.

HOW TO REQUEST AN ACTIVE DUTY ALERT

STEP BY STEP:	NOTES:		
☐ Contact **1** credit reporting company.	*Equifax* *1-800-525-6285*	*Experian* *1-888-397-3742*	*TransUnion* *1-800-680-7289*
	☐ Request an active duty alert. ☐ Provide proof of identity, like a government-issued identity card, driver's license, military identification, birth certificate, or passport. *The company you call must contact the others.* *The credit reporting companies will take your name off their marketing list for prescreened credit card offers for 2 years, unless you ask them to add you back onto the list.*		
☐ Mark your calendar.	*Active duty alerts last for 1 year. If your deployment lasts longer, renew the alert.*		
☐ Update your files.	☐ Record the dates you made calls or sent letters. ☐ Keep copies of letters in your files.		

Protect Your Personal Information

Keep your important papers secure

- **Lock them up.** Lock your financial documents and records in a safe place at home, and lock your wallet or purse in a safe place at work. Keep your information secure from roommates or workers who come into your home.

- **Limit what you carry.** When you go out, take only the identification, credit, and debit cards you need. Leave your Social Security and Medicare cards at home or in a secure place.

- **Pick up your new checks at the bank.** When you order new checks, don't have them mailed to your home, unless you have a secure mailbox with a lock.

- **Be careful with your mail.** Take outgoing mail to post office collection boxes or the post office. Promptly remove mail that arrives in your mailbox. If you will be away from home for several days, request a vacation hold on your mail:

  - go to your local post office,

  - visit www.usps.com/holdmail, or

  - call the U.S. Postal Service at 1-800-275-8777

- **Shred sensitive documents.** Shred receipts, credit offers, credit applications, insurance forms, physician statements, checks, bank statements, expired charge cards, and similar documents before you put them in your trash.

- **Consider opting out of prescreened offers of credit** and insurance by mail. You can opt out for 5 years or permanently. To opt out for 5 years, call 1-888-567-8688 or go to www.optoutprescreen.com. The 3 nationwide credit reporting companies operate the phone number and website.

- **Protect your medical information.** Destroy the labels on prescription bottles before you throw them out. Don't share your health plan information with anyone who offers free health services or products.

- **Exercise your curiosity.** Before you share information at your workplace, a business, your child's school, or a doctor's office, ask who will have access to your information, how it will be handled, and how it will be disposed of.

Secure your Social Security Number

- **Protect it.** Share your Social Security number, and your child's, only when necessary. Ask if you can use a different kind of identification.

- **If someone asks you to share** your Social Security number or your child's, ask:

  - why they need it

  - how it will be used

  - how they will protect it

  - what happens if you don't share the number

  The decision to share is yours. A business may not provide you with a service or benefit if you don't provide your number.

- **Sometimes you must share your number**. Your employer and financial institutions need your Social Security number for wage and tax reporting purposes. A business may ask for your Social Security number so they can check your credit when you apply for a loan, rent an apartment, or sign up for utility service.

Be alert to impersonators online

- **Be sure you know who is getting your personal or financial information online.** If a company that claims to have an account with you sends email asking for personal information, don't click on links in the email. Instead, type the company name into your web browser, go to their site, and contact them through customer service. Or, call the customer service number listed on your account statement. Ask whether the company really sent a request.

Protect your computer and mobile device

- **Use anti-virus software, anti-spyware software, and a firewall.** Set your preference to update these protections often. Protect against intrusions and infections that can compromise your computer files or passwords by installing security patches for your operating system and other software programs.

- **Don't open files, click on links, or download programs sent by strangers.** Opening a file from someone you don't know could expose your system to a computer virus or spyware that captures your passwords or other information you type.

- **Safely dispose of personal information**.

  - Before you dispose of a computer, get rid of all the personal information it stores. Use a wipe utility program to overwrite the entire hard drive.

- Before you dispose of a mobile device:
  - Check your owner's manual, the service provider's website, or the device manufacturer's website for information on how to delete information permanently, and how to save or transfer information to a new device.
  - Remove the memory or subscriber identity module (SIM) card from a mobile device. Remove the phone book, lists of calls made and received, voicemails, messages sent and received, organizer folders, web search history, and photos.

Protect your data and personal information

- **Encrypt your data.** Keep your browser secure. To guard your online transactions, use encryption software that scrambles information you send over the internet. A "lock" icon on the status bar of your internet browser means your information will be safe when it's transmitted. Look for the lock before you send personal or financial information online.

- **Be wise about Wi-Fi.** Before you send personal information over your laptop or smartphone on a public wireless network in a coffee shop, library, airport, hotel, or other public place, see if your information will be protected. If you use an encrypted website, it protects only the information you send to and from that site. If you use a secure wireless network, all the information you send on that network is protected.

- **Keep passwords private.** Use strong passwords with your laptop, credit, bank and other accounts. The longer the password, the harder it is to crack. Create passwords that mix letters, numbers, and special characters. Don't use the same password for many accounts. If it's stolen from you – or from one of the companies with which you do business – it can be used to take over all your accounts.

- **Don't overshare on social networking sites.** If you post too much information about yourself, an identity thief can find information about your life, use it to answer 'challenge' questions on your accounts, and get access to your money and personal information. Consider limiting access to your networking page to a small group of people. Never post your full name, Social Security number, address, phone number, or account numbers in publicly accessible sites.

- **Lock up your laptop**. Keep financial information on your laptop only when necessary. Don't use an automatic login feature that saves your user name and password, and always log off when you're finished. That way, if your laptop is stolen, it will be harder for a thief to get at your personal information.

- **Read privacy policies.** Yes, they can be long and complex, but they tell you how the site maintains accuracy, access, security, and control of the personal information it collects; how it uses the information, and whether it provides information to third parties. If you don't see or understand a site's privacy policy, consider doing business elsewhere.

SAMPLE LETTERS AND FORMS

Sample Letters

Enclosures

Forms

For more sample letters and forms, see www.ftc.gov/idtheft.

SAMPLE DISPUTE LETTER FOR EXISTING ACCOUNTS

[Date]

[Your Name]
[Your Address]
[Your City, State, Zip Code]

[Name of Company]
[Fraud Department or Billing Inquiries]
[Address]
[City, State, Zip Code]

[RE: Your Account Number (if known)]

Dear Sir or Madam:

I am writing to dispute [a] fraudulent charge[s] on my account in the amount[s] of $_____, and posted on [dates]. I am a victim of identity theft, and I did not make [this/these] charge[s]. I request that you remove the fraudulent charge[s] and any related finance charge and other charges from my account, send me an updated and accurate statement, and close the account (if applicable). I also request that you stop reporting this inaccurate information and report the correct information to all of the nationwide credit reporting companies (CRCs) to which you provided it.

Enclosed is a copy of my Identity Theft Report, credit report, and account statement showing the fraudulent items related to your company that are the result of identity theft. Also enclosed is a copy of the Notice to Furnishers of Information issued by the Federal Trade Commission, which details your responsibilities under the Fair Credit Reporting Act as an information furnisher to CRCs.

Please investigate this matter and send me a written explanation of your findings and actions.

Sincerely,
[Your Name]

Enclosures:

- Identity Theft Report
- Proof of Identity
- FTC Notice to Furnishers of Information
- Copy of account statement showing fraudulent items
- Credit report of [Your Name] identifying information to be corrected

SAMPLE DISPUTE LETTER FOR NEW ACCOUNTS

[Date]

[Your Name]
[Your Address]
[Your City, State, Zip Code]

[Name of Company]
[Fraud Department or Billing Inquiries]
[Address]
[City, State, Zip Code]

[RE: Your Account Number (if known)]

Dear Sir or Madam:

I am a victim of identity theft. I recently learned that my personal information was used to open an account at your company. I did not open or authorize this account, and I therefore request that it be closed immediately. I also request that [Company Name] absolve me of all charges on the account, and that you take all appropriate steps to remove information about this account from my credit files.

Enclosed is a copy of my Identity Theft Report, and a copy of my credit report showing the fraudulent items related to your company that are the result of identity theft. Also enclosed is a copy of the Federal Trade Commission Notice to Furnishers of Information, which details your responsibilities as an information furnisher to credit reporting companies (CRCs). As a furnisher, upon receipt of a consumer's written request that encloses an Identity Theft Report, you are required to cease furnishing the information resulting from identity theft to any credit reporting company.

The Notice also specifies your responsibilities when you receive notice from a CRC, under section 605B of the Fair Credit Reporting Act, that information you provided to the CRC may be the result of identity theft. Those responsibilities include ceasing to provide the inaccurate information to any CRC and ensuring that you do not attempt to sell or transfer the fraudulent debts to another party for collection.

Please investigate this matter, close the account and absolve me of all charges, take the steps required under the Fair Credit Reporting Act, and send me a letter explaining your findings and actions.

Sincerely,
[Your Name]

Enclosures:

- Identity Theft Report
- FTC Notice to Furnishers of Information
- Credit report of [Your Name] identifying information to be corrected

SAMPLE DISPUTE LETTER TO CREDIT REPORTING COMPANY

[Date]

[Your Name]
[Your Address]
[Your City, State, Zip Code]

[Credit Reporting Company Name and Address]
Write a separate letter to each of the 3 companies.
See contact info on inside back cover.

Dear Sir or Madam:

I am a victim of identity theft and I write to dispute certain information in my file resulting from the crime. I have circled the items I dispute on the attached copy of my credit report. The items I am disputing do not relate to any transactions that I made or authorized. Please remove or correct this information at the earliest possible time.

I dispute the [name of source, like "Company" or "Court"] [name of item, like "account" or "judgment"] because [explain why the item is inaccurate]. As required by section 611 of the Fair Credit Reporting Act, a copy of which is enclosed, I am requesting that the item[s] be removed [or request another specific change] to correct the information.

[If possible: I have enclosed copies of documents that support my dispute.]

Please investigate and correct the disputed item[s] as soon as possible.

Sincerely,

[Your Name]

Enclosures:

- Identity Theft Report
- Credit report of [Your Name] identifying information to be corrected
- FCRA Section 611

MEMO FROM FTC TO LAW ENFORCEMENT

To: Law Enforcement Officer

From: Division of Privacy and Identity Protection
The Federal Trade Commission

Re: **Importance of Identity Theft Report**

The purpose of this memorandum is to explain what an "Identity Theft Report" is, and its importance to identity theft victims in helping them to recover. A police report that contains specific details of an identity theft is considered an "Identity Theft Report" under section 605B of the Fair Credit Reporting Act (FCRA), and it entitles an identity theft victim to certain important protections that can help him or her recover more quickly from identity theft.

Specifically, under sections 605B, 615(f) and 623(a)(6) of the FCRA, an Identity Theft Report can be used to permanently block fraudulent information that results from identity theft, such as accounts or addresses, from appearing on a victim's credit report. It will also make sure these debts do not reappear on the credit reports. Identity Theft Reports can prevent a company from continuing to collect debts that result from identity theft, or selling them to others for collection. An Identity Theft Report is also needed to allow an identity theft victim to place an extended fraud alert on his or her credit report.

In order for a police report to be incorporated in an Identity Theft Report, and therefore entitle an identity theft victim to the protections discussed above, the police report must contain details about the accounts and inaccurate information that resulted from the identity theft. We advise victims to bring a printed copy of their ID Theft Complaint filed with the FTC with them to the police station in order to better assist you in creating a detailed police report so that these victims can access the important protections available to them if they have an Identity Theft Report. The victim should sign the ID Theft Complaint in your presence. If possible, you should attach or incorporate the ID Theft Complaint into the police report, and sign the "Law Enforcement Report Information" section of the FTC's ID Theft Complaint. In addition, please provide the identity theft victim with a copy of the Identity Theft Report (the police report with the victim's ID Theft Complaint attached or incorporated) to permit the victim to dispute the fraudulent accounts and debts created by the identity thief.

For additional information on Identity Theft Reports or identity theft, please visit www.ftc.gov/idtheft.

FCRA § 611 (15 U.S.C. § 1681I)
PROCEDURE IN CASE OF DISPUTED ACCURACY

(a) Reinvestigations of Disputed Information

  (1) Reinvestigation Required

    (A) In general. Subject to subsection (f), if the completeness or accuracy of any item of information contained in a consumer's file at a consumer reporting agency is disputed by the consumer and the consumer notifies the agency directly, or indirectly through a reseller, of such dispute, the agency shall, free of charge, conduct a reasonable reinvestigation to determine whether the disputed information is inaccurate and record the current status of the disputed information, or delete the item from the file in accordance with paragraph (5), before the end of the 30-day period beginning on the date on which the agency receives the notice of the dispute from the consumer or reseller.

    (B) Extension of period to reinvestigate. Except as provided in subparagraph (C), the 30-day period described in subparagraph (A) may be extended for not more than 15 additional days if the consumer reporting agency receives information from the consumer during that 30-day period that is relevant to the reinvestigation.

    (C) Limitations on extension of period to reinvestigate. Subparagraph (B) shall not apply to any reinvestigation in which, during the 30-day period described in subparagraph (A), the information that is the subject of the reinvestigation is found to be inaccurate or incomplete or the consumer reporting agency determines that the information cannot be verified.

  (2) Prompt Notice of Dispute to Furnisher of Information

    (A) In general. Before the expiration of the 5-business-day period beginning on the date on which a consumer reporting agency receives notice of a dispute from any consumer or a reseller in accordance with paragraph (1), the agency shall provide notification of the dispute to any person who provided any item of information in dispute, at the address and in the manner established with the person. The notice shall include all relevant information regarding the dispute that the agency has received from the consumer or reseller.

    (B) Provision of other information. The consumer reporting agency shall promptly provide to the person who provided the information in dispute all relevant information regarding the dispute that is received by the agency from the consumer or the reseller after the period referred to in subparagraph (A) and before the end of the period referred to in paragraph (1) (A).

  (3) Determination That Dispute Is Frivolous or Irrelevant

    (A) In general. Notwithstanding paragraph (1), a consumer reporting agency may terminate a reinvestigation of information disputed by a consumer under that paragraph if the agency reasonably determines that the dispute by the consumer is frivolous or irrelevant, including by reason of a failure by a consumer to provide sufficient information to investigate the disputed information.

    (B) Notice of determination. Upon making any determination in accordance with subparagraph (A) that a dispute is frivolous or irrelevant, a consumer reporting agency shall notify the consumer of such determination not later than 5 business days after making such determination, by mail or, if authorized by the consumer for that purpose, by any other means available to the agency.

    (C) Contents of notice. A notice under subparagraph (B) shall include

      (i) the reasons for the determination under subparagraph (A); and

      (ii) identification of any information required to investigate the disputed information, which may consist of a standardized form describing the general nature of such information.

(4) Consideration of consumer information. In conducting any reinvestigation under paragraph (1) with respect to disputed information in the file of any consumer, the consumer reporting agency shall review and consider all relevant information submitted by the consumer in the period described in paragraph (1)(A) with respect to such disputed information.

(5) Treatment of Inaccurate or Unverifiable Information

(A) In general. If, after any reinvestigation under paragraph (1) of any information disputed by a consumer, an item of the information is found to be inaccurate or incomplete or cannot be verified, the consumer reporting agency shall—

(i) promptly delete that item of information from the file of the consumer, or modify that item of information, as appropriate, based on the results of the reinvestigation; and

(ii) promptly notify the furnisher of that information that the information has been modified or deleted from the file of the consumer.

(B) Requirements Relating to Reinsertion of Previously Deleted Material

(i) Certification of accuracy of information. If any information is deleted from a consumer's file pursuant to subparagraph (A), the information may not be reinserted in the file by the consumer reporting agency

unless the person who furnishes the information certifies that the information is complete and accurate.

(ii) Notice to consumer. If any information that has been deleted from a consumer's file pursuant to subparagraph (A) is reinserted in the file, the consumer reporting agency shall notify the consumer of the reinsertion in writing not later than 5 business days after the reinsertion or, if authorized by the consumer for that purpose, by any other means available to the agency.

(iii) Additional information. As part of, or in addition to, the notice under clause (ii), a consumer reporting agency shall provide to a consumer in writing not later than 5 business days after the date of the reinsertion

(I) a statement that the disputed information has been reinserted;

(II) the business name and address of any furnisher of information contacted and the telephone number of such furnisher, if reasonably available, or of any furnisher of information that contacted the consumer reporting agency, in connection with the reinsertion of such information; and

(III) a notice that the consumer has the right to add a statement to the consumer's file disputing the accuracy or completeness of the disputed information.

(C) Procedures to prevent reappearance. A consumer reporting agency shall maintain reasonable procedures designed to prevent the reappearance in a consumer's file, and in consumer reports on the consumer, of information that is deleted pursuant to this paragraph (other than information that is reinserted in accordance with subparagraph (B)(i)).

(D) Automated reinvestigation system. Any consumer reporting agency that compiles and maintains files on consumers on a nationwide basis shall implement an automated system through which furnishers of information to that consumer reporting agency may report the results of a reinvestigation that finds incomplete or inaccurate information in a consumer's file to other such consumer reporting agencies.

(6) Notice of Results of Reinvestigation

(A) In general. A consumer reporting agency shall provide written notice to a consumer of the results of a reinvestigation under this subsection not later than 5 business days after the completion of the reinvestigation, by mail or, if authorized by the consumer for that purpose, by other means available to the agency.

(B) Contents. As part of, or in addition to, the notice under subparagraph (A), a consumer reporting agency shall provide to a consumer in writing before the expiration of the 5-day period referred to in subparagraph (A)

(i) a statement that the reinvestigation is completed;

(ii) a consumer report that is based upon the consumer's file as that file is revised as a result of the reinvestigation;

(iii) a notice that, if requested by the consumer, a description of the procedure used to determine the accuracy and completeness of the information shall be provided to the consumer by the agency, including the business name and address of any furnisher of information contacted in connection with such information and the telephone number of such furnisher, if reasonably available;

(iv) a notice that the consumer has the right to add a statement to the consumer's file disputing the accuracy or completeness of the information; and

(v) a notice that the consumer has the right to request under subsection (d) that the consumer reporting agency furnish notifications under that subsection.

(7) Description of reinvestigation procedure. A consumer reporting agency shall provide to a consumer a description referred to in paragraph (6)(B)(iii) by not later than 15 days after receiving a request from the consumer for that description.

(8) Expedited dispute resolution. If a dispute regarding an item of information in a consumer's file at a consumer reporting agency is resolved in accordance with paragraph (5)(A) by the deletion of the disputed information by not later than 3 business days after the date on which the agency receives notice of the dispute from the consumer in accordance with paragraph (1)(A), then the agency shall not be required to comply with paragraphs (2), (6), and (7) with respect to that dispute if the agency

(A) provides prompt notice of the deletion to the consumer by telephone;

(B) includes in that notice, or in a written notice that accompanies a confirmation and consumer report provided in accordance with subparagraph (C), a statement of the consumer's right to request under subsection (d) that the agency furnish notifications under that subsection; and

(C) provides written confirmation of the deletion and a copy of a consumer report on the consumer that is based on the consumer's file after the deletion, not later than 5 business days after making the deletion.

(b) Statement of dispute. If the reinvestigation does not resolve the dispute, the consumer may file a brief statement setting forth the nature of the dispute. The consumer reporting agency may limit such statements to not more than one hundred words if it provides the consumer with assistance in writing a clear summary of the dispute.

(c) Notification of consumer dispute in subsequent consumer reports. Whenever a statement of a dispute is filed, unless there is reasonable grounds to believe that it is frivolous or irrelevant, the consumer reporting agency shall, in any subsequent report containing the information in question, clearly note that it is disputed by the consumer and provide either the consumer's statement or a clear and accurate codification or summary thereof.

(d) Notification of deletion of disputed information. Following any deletion of information which is found to be inaccurate or whose accuracy can no longer be verified or any notation as to disputed information, the consumer reporting agency shall, at the request of the consumer, furnish notification that the item has been deleted or the statement, codification or summary pursuant to subsection (b) or (c) of this section to any person specifically designated by the consumer who has within two years prior thereto received a consumer report for employment purposes, or within six months prior thereto received a consumer report for any other purpose, which contained the deleted or disputed information.

(e) Treatment of Complaints and Report to Congress

(1) In general. The Commission shall-

(A) compile all complaints that it receives that a file of a consumer that is maintained by a consumer reporting agency described in section 603(p) contains incomplete or inaccurate information, with respect to which, the consumer appears to have disputed the completeness or accuracy with the consumer reporting agency or otherwise utilized the procedures provided by subsection (a); and

(B) transmit each such complaint to each consumer reporting agency involved.

(2) Exclusion. Complaints received or obtained by the Commission pursuant to its investigative authority under the Federal Trade Commission Act shall not be subject to paragraph (1).

(3) Agency responsibilities. Each consumer reporting agency described in section 603(p) that receives a complaint transmitted by the Commission pursuant to paragraph (1) shall-

(A) review each such complaint to determine whether all legal obligations imposed on the consumer reporting agency under this title (including any obligation imposed by an applicable court or administrative order) have been met with respect to the subject matter of the complaint;

(B) provide reports on a regular basis to the Commission regarding the determinations of and actions taken by the consumer reporting agency, if any, in connection with its review of such complaints; and

(C) maintain, for a reasonable time period, records regarding the disposition of each such complaint that is sufficient to demonstrate compliance with this subsection.

(4) Rulemaking authority. The Commission may prescribe regulations, as appropriate to implement this subsection.

(5) Annual report. The Commission shall submit to the Committee on Banking, Housing, and Urban Affairs of the Senate and the Committee on Financial Services of the House of Representatives an annual report regarding information gathered by the Commission under this subsection.'.

(f) Reinvestigation Requirement Applicable to Resellers

(1) Exemption from general reinvestigation requirement. Except as provided in paragraph (2), a reseller shall be exempt from the requirements of this section.

(2) Action required upon receiving notice of a dispute. If a reseller receives a notice from a consumer of a dispute concerning the completeness or accuracy of any item of information contained in a consumer report on such consumer produced by the reseller, the reseller shall, within 5 business days of receiving the notice, and free of charge–

(A) determine whether the item of information is incomplete or inaccurate as a result of an act or omission of the reseller; and

(B) if (i) the reseller determines that the item of information is incomplete or inaccurate as a result of an act or omission of the reseller, not later than 20 days after receiving the notice, correct the information in the consumer report or delete it; or

(ii) if the reseller determines that the item of information is not incomplete or inaccurate as a result of an act or omission of the reseller, convey the notice of the dispute, together with all relevant information provided by the consumer, to each consumer reporting agency that provided the reseller with the information that is the subject of the dispute, using an address or a notification mechanism specified by the consumer reporting agency for such notices.

(3) Responsibility of consumer reporting agency to notify consumer through reseller. Upon the completion of a reinvestigation under this section of a dispute concerning the completeness or accuracy of any information in the file of a consumer by a consumer reporting agency that received notice of the dispute from a reseller under paragraph (2)-

(A) the notice by the consumer reporting agency under paragraph (6), (7), or (8) of subsection (a) shall be provided to the reseller in lieu of the consumer; and

(B) the reseller shall immediately reconvey such notice to the consumer, including any notice of a deletion by telephone in the manner required under paragraph (8)(A).

(4) Reseller reinvestigations. No provision of this subsection shall be construed as prohibiting a reseller from conducting a reinvestigation of a consumer dispute directly.

All furnishers subject to the Federal Trade Commission's jurisdiction must comply with all applicable regulations, including regulations promulgated after this notice was prescribed in 2004. Information about applicable regulations currently in effect can be found at the Commission's Web site, www.ftc.gov/credit. Furnishers who are not subject to the Commission's jurisdiction should consult with their regulators to find any relevant regulations.

NOTICE TO FURNISHERS OF INFORMATION:
OBLIGATIONS OF FURNISHERS UNDER THE FCRA

The federal Fair Credit Reporting Act (FCRA), 15 U.S.C. 1681-1681y, imposes responsibilities on all persons who furnish information to consumer reporting agencies (CRAs). These responsibilities are found in Section 623 of the FCRA, 15 U.S.C. 1681s-2. State law may impose additional requirements on furnishers. All furnishers of information to CRAs should become familiar with the applicable laws and may want to consult with their counsel to ensure that they are in compliance. The text of the FCRA is set forth in full at the Web-site of the Federal Trade Commission (FTC): www.ftc.gov/credit. A list of the sections of the FCRA crossreferenced to the U.S. Code is at the end of this document.

Section 623 imposes the following duties upon furnishers:

ACCURACY GUIDELINES
The banking and credit union regulators and the FTC will promulgate guidelines and regulations dealing with the accuracy of information provided to CRAs by furnishers. The regulations and guidelines issued by the FTC will be available at www.ftc.gov/credit when they are issued. Section 623(e).

GENERAL PROHIBITION ON REPORTING INACCURATE INFORMATION
The FCRA prohibits information furnishers from providing information to a CRA that they know or have reasonable cause to believe is inaccurate. However, the furnisher is not subject to this general prohibition if it clearly and conspicuously specifies an address to which consumers may write to notify the furnisher that certain information is inaccurate. Sections 623(a)(1)(A) and (a)(1)(C).

DUTY TO CORRECT AND UPDATE INFORMATION
If at any time a person who regularly and in the ordinary course of business furnishes information to one or more CRAs determines that the information provided is not complete or accurate, the furnisher must promptly provide complete and accurate information to the CRA. In addition, the furnisher must notify all CRAs that received the information of any corrections, and must thereafter report only the complete and accurate information. Section 623(a)(2).

DUTIES AFTER NOTICE OF DISPUTE FROM CONSUMER
If a consumer notifies a furnisher, at an address specified for the furnisher for such notices, that specific information is inaccurate, and the information is, in fact, inaccurate, the furnisher must thereafter report the correct information to CRAs. Section 623(a)(1)(B).

If a consumer notifies a furnisher that the consumer disputes the completeness or accuracy of any information reported by the furnisher, the furnisher may not subsequently report that information to a CRA without providing notice of the dispute. Section 623(a)(3).

The federal banking and credit union regulators and the FTC will issue regulations that will identify when an information furnisher must investigate a dispute made directly to the furnisher by a consumer. Once these regulations are issued, furnishers must comply with them and complete an investigation within 30 days (or 45 days, if the consumer later provides relevant additional information) unless the dispute is frivolous or irrelevant or comes from a "credit repair organization." The FTC regulations will be available at www.ftc.gov/credit. Section 623(a)(8).

DUTIES AFTER NOTICE OF DISPUTE FROM CONSUMER REPORTING AGENCY
If a CRA notifies a furnisher that a consumer disputes the completeness or accuracy of information provided by the furnisher, the furnisher has a duty to follow certain procedures. The furnisher must:

- Conduct an investigation and review all relevant information provided by the CRA, including information given to the CRA by the consumer. Sections 623(b)(1)(A) and (b)(1)(B).

- Report the results to the CRA that referred the dispute, and, if the investigation establishes that the information was, in fact, incomplete or inaccurate, report the results to all CRAs to which the furnisher provided the information that compile and maintain files on a nationwide basis. Section 623(b)(1)(C) and (b)(1)(D).

- Complete the above steps within 30 days from the date the CRA receives the dispute (or 45 days, if the consumer later provides relevant additional information to the CRA). Section 623(b)(2).

- Promptly modify or delete the information, or block its reporting. Section 623(b)(1)(E).

DUTY TO REPORT VOLUNTARY CLOSING OF CREDIT ACCOUNTS
If a consumer voluntarily closes a credit account, any person who regularly and in the ordinary course of business furnishes information to one or more CRAs must report this fact when it provides information to CRAs for the time period in which the account was closed. Section 623(a)(4).

DUTY TO REPORT DATES OF DELINQUENCIES
If a furnisher reports information concerning a delinquent account placed for collection, charged to profit or loss, or subject to any similar action, the furnisher must, within 90 days after reporting the information, provide the CRA with the month and the year of the commencement of the delinquency that immediately preceded the action, so that the agency will know how long to keep the information in the consumer's file. Section 623(a)(5).

Any person, such as a debt collector, that has acquired or is responsible for collecting delinquent accounts and that reports information to CRAs may comply with the requirements of Section 623(a)(5) (until there is a consumer dispute) by reporting the same delinquency date previously reported by the creditor. If the creditor did not report this date, they may comply with the FCRA by establishing reasonable procedures to obtain and report delinquency dates, or, if a delinquency date cannot be reasonably obtained, by following reasonable procedures to ensure that the date reported precedes the date when the account was placed for collection, charged to profit or loss, or subjected to any similar action. Section 623(a)(5).

DUTIES OF FINANCIAL INSTITUTIONS WHEN REPORTING NEGATIVE INFORMATION
Financial institutions that furnish information to "nationwide" consumer reporting agencies, as defined in Section 603(p), must notify consumers in writing if they may furnish or have furnished negative information to a CRA. Section 623(a)(7). The Federal Reserve Board has prescribed model disclosures, 12 CFR Part 222, App. B.

DUTIES WHEN FURNISHING MEDICAL INFORMATION
A furnisher whose primary business is providing medical services, products, or devices (and such furnisher's agents or assignees) is a medical information furnisher for the purposes of the FCRA and must notify all CRAs to which it reports of this fact. Section 623(a)(9). This notice will enable CRAs to comply with their duties under Section 604(g) when reporting medical information.

DUTIES WHEN ID THEFT OCCURS
All furnishers must have in place reasonable procedures to respond to notifications from CRAs that information furnished is the result of identity theft, and to prevent refurnishing the information in the future. A furnisher may not furnish information that a consumer has identified as resulting from identity theft unless the furnisher subsequently knows or is informed by the consumer that the information is correct. Section 623(a)(6). If a furnisher learns that it has furnished inaccurate information due to identity theft, it must notify each consumer reporting agency of the correct information and must thereafter report only complete and accurate information. Section 623(a)(2). When any furnisher of information is notified pursuant to the procedures set forth in Section 605B that a debt has resulted from identity theft, the furnisher may not sell, transfer, or place for collection the debt except in certain limited circumstances. Section 615(f).

The FTC's Web site, www.ftc.gov/credit, has more information about the FCRA, including publications for businesses and the full text of the FCRA.

Annual Credit Report Request Form

You have the right to get a free copy of your credit file disclosure, commonly called a credit report, once every 12 months, from each of the nationwide consumer credit reporting companies - Equifax, Experian and TransUnion.

For instant access to your free credit report, visit www.annualcreditreport.com.

For more information on obtaining your free credit report, visit www.annualcreditreport.com or call 877-322-8228.

Use this form if you prefer to write to request your credit report from any, or all, of the nationwide consumer credit reporting companies. The following information is required to process your request. **Omission of any information may delay your request.**

Once complete, fold (do not staple or tape), place into a #10 envelope, affix required postage and mail to:
Annual Credit Report Request Service P.O. Box 105281 Atlanta, GA 30348-5281.

Please use a Black or Blue Pen and write your responses in PRINTED CAPITAL LETTERS without touching the sides of the boxes like the examples listed below:

A B C D E F G H I J K L M N O P Q R S T U V W X Y Z   0 1 2 3 4 5 6 7 8 9

Social Security Number:

Date of Birth:

Month / Day / Year

---Fold Here---   ---Fold Here---

First Name   M.I.

Last Name   JR, SR, III, etc.

Current Mailing Address:

House Number   **Street Name**

Apartment Number / Private Mailbox   **For Puerto Rico Only: Print Urbanization Name**

City   **State**   **ZipCode**

Previous Mailing Address (complete only if at current mailing address for less than two years):

House Number   **Street Name**

---Fold Here---   ---Fold Here---

Apartment Number / Private Mailbox   **For Puerto Rico Only: Print Urbanization Name**

City   **State**   **ZipCode**

Shade Circle Like This → ●

Not Like This → ⊗ ☑

I want a credit report from (shade each that you would like to receive):
- ○ Equifax
- ○ Experian
- ○ TransUnion

○ **Shade here if, for security reasons, you want your credit report to include no more than the last four digits of your Social Security Number.**

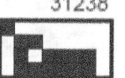

31238

If additional information is needed to process your request, the consumer credit reporting company will contact you by mail.

Your request will be processed within 15 days of receipt and then mailed to you.

Copyright 2004, Central Source LLC

G-1

Identity Theft Victim's Complaint and Affidavit

A voluntary form for filing a report with law enforcement, and disputes with credit reporting agencies and creditors about identity theft-related problems. Visit ftc.gov/idtheft to use a secure online version that you can print for your records.

Before completing this form:
1. Place a fraud alert on your credit reports, and review the reports for signs of fraud.
2. Close the accounts that you know, or believe, have been tampered with or opened fraudulently.

About You *(the victim)*

Now

(1)　My full legal name: _____
　　　　　　　　　　　　　　　　　First　　　　Middle　　　　Last　　　　Suffix

(2)　My date of birth: _____
　　　　　　　　　　　　　　mm/dd/yyyy

(3)　My Social Security number: _____ - _____ - _____

(4)　My driver's license: _____　_____
　　　　　　　　　　　　　　　　　State　　　　　Number

(5)　My current street address:

　　　_____
　　　　　Number & Street Name　　　　　　　　Apartment, Suite, etc.

　　　_____
　　　　　City　　　　　State　　　　Zip Code　　　　Country

(6)　I have lived at this address since _____
　　　　　　　　　　　　　　　　　　　　　　　　mm/yyyy

(7)　My daytime phone: (____)_____
　　　My evening phone: (____)_____
　　　My email: _____

> Leave (3) blank until you provide this form to someone with a legitimate business need, like when you are filing your report at the police station or sending the form to a credit reporting agency to correct your credit report.

At the Time of the Fraud

(8)　My full legal name was: _____
　　　　　　　　　　　　　　　　　First　　　Middle　　　Last　　　Suffix

(9)　My address was: _____
　　　　　　　　　　　Number & Street Name　　　　Apartment, Suite, etc.

　　　_____
　　　　　City　　　　　State　　　　Zip Code　　　　Country

(10)　My daytime phone: (____)_____　My evening phone: (____)_____
　　　My email: _____

> Skip (8) - (10) if your information has not changed since the fraud.

The Paperwork Reduction Act requires the FTC to display a valid control number (in this case, OMB control #3084-0047) before we can collect — or sponsor the collection of — your information, or require you to provide it.

About You *(the victim)* *(Continued)*

Declarations

(11) I ☐ did OR ☐ did not authorize anyone to use my name or personal information to obtain money, credit, loans, goods, or services — or for any other purpose — as described in this report.

(12) I ☐ did OR ☐ did not receive any money, goods, services, or other benefit as a result of the events described in this report.

(13) I ☐ am OR ☐ am not willing to work with law enforcement if charges are brought against the person(s) who committed the fraud.

About the Fraud

(14) I believe the following person used my information or identification documents to open new accounts, use my existing accounts, or commit other fraud.

| **(14):** Enter what you know about anyone you believe was involved (even if you don't have complete information). |

Name: _____
First   Middle   Last   Suffix

Address: _____
Number & Street Name   Apartment, Suite, etc.

_____
City   State   Zip Code   Country

Phone Numbers: (_____)_____ (_____)_____

Additional information about this person: _____

_____

_____

_____

_____

_____

_____

_____

_____

_____

_____

_____

(15) Additional information about the crime (for example, how the identity thief gained access to your information or which documents or information were used):

_____

_____

_____

_____

_____

_____

_____

> (14) and (15): Attach additional sheets as needed.

Documentation

(16) I can verify my identity with these documents:

☐ A valid government-issued photo identification card (for example, my driver's license, state-issued ID card, or my passport).
If you are under 16 and don't have a photo-ID, a copy of your birth certificate or a copy of your official school record showing your enrollment and legal address is acceptable.

☐ Proof of residency during the time the disputed charges occurred, the loan was made, or the other event took place (for example, a copy of a rental/lease agreement in my name, a utility bill, or an insurance bill).

> (16): Reminder: Attach copies of your identity documents when sending this form to creditors and credit reporting agencies.

About the Information or Accounts

(17) The following personal information (like my name, address, Social Security number, or date of birth) in my credit report is inaccurate as a result of this identity theft:

(A) _____

(B) _____

(C) _____

(18) Credit inquiries from these companies appear on my credit report as a result of this identity theft:

Company Name: _____

Company Name: _____

Company Name: _____

(19)   Below are details about the different frauds committed using my personal information.

Name of Institution _____   Contact Person _____   Phone _____   Extension _____

Account Number _____   Routing Number _____   Affected Check Number(s) _____

Account Type: ☐ Credit   ☐ Bank   ☐ Phone/Utilities   ☐ Loan
☐ Government Benefits   ☐ Internet or Email   ☐ Other

Select ONE:
☐ This account was opened fraudulently.
☐ This was an existing account that someone tampered with.

Date Opened or Misused (mm/yyyy) _____   Date Discovered (mm/yyyy) _____   Total Amount Obtained ($) _____

Name of Institution _____   Contact Person _____   Phone _____   Extension _____

Account Number _____   Routing Number _____   Affected Check Number(s) _____

Account Type: ☐ Credit   ☐ Bank   ☐ Phone/Utilities   ☐ Loan
☐ Government Benefits   ☐ Internet or Email   ☐ Other

Select ONE:
☐ This account was opened fraudulently.
☐ This was an existing account that someone tampered with.

Date Opened or Misused (mm/yyyy) _____   Date Discovered (mm/yyyy) _____   Total Amount Obtained ($) _____

Name of Institution _____   Contact Person _____   Phone _____   Extension _____

Account Number _____   Routing Number _____   Affected Check Number(s) _____

Account Type: ☐ Credit   ☐ Bank   ☐ Phone/Utilities   ☐ Loan
☐ Government Benefits   ☐ Internet or Email   ☐ Other

Select ONE:
☐ This account was opened fraudulently.
☐ This was an existing account that someone tampered with.

Date Opened or Misused (mm/yyyy) _____   Date Discovered (mm/yyyy) _____   Total Amount Obtained ($) _____

---

(19):
If there were more than three frauds, copy this page blank, and attach as many additional copies as necessary.

Enter any applicable information that you have, even if it is incomplete or an estimate.

If the thief committed two types of fraud at one company, list the company twice, giving the information about the two frauds separately.

Contact Person: Someone you dealt with, whom an investigator can call about this fraud.

Account Number: The number of the credit or debit card, bank account, loan, or other account that was misused.

Dates: Indicate when the thief began to misuse your information and when you discovered the problem.

Amount Obtained: For instance, the total amount purchased with the card or withdrawn from the account.

Your Law Enforcement Report

(20)   One way to get a credit reporting agency to quickly block identity theft-related information from appearing on your credit report is to submit a detailed law enforcement report ("Identity Theft Report"). You can obtain an Identity Theft Report by taking this form to your local law enforcement office, along with your supporting documentation. Ask an officer to witness your signature and complete the rest of the information in this section. It's important to get your report number, whether or not you are able to file in person or get a copy of the official law enforcement report. Attach a copy of any confirmation letter or official law enforcement report you receive when sending this form to credit reporting agencies.

Select ONE:

☐ I have not filed a law enforcement report.

☐ I was unable to file any law enforcement report.

☐ I filed an automated report with the law enforcement agency listed below.

☐ I filed my report in person with the law enforcement officer and agency listed below.

_____	_____
Law Enforcement Department	State

_____	_____
Report Number	Filing Date (mm/dd/yyyy)

_____	_____
Officer's Name (please print)	Officer's Signature

_____	(____)_____
Badge Number	Phone Number

Did the victim receive a copy of the report from the law enforcement officer?   ☐ Yes OR ☐ No

Victim's FTC complaint number (if available): _____

(20):
Check "I have not..." if you have not yet filed a report with law enforcement or you have chosen not to. Check "I was unable..." if you tried to file a report but law enforcement refused to take it.

Automated report: A law enforcement report filed through an automated system, for example, by telephone, mail, or the Internet, instead of a face-to-face interview with a law enforcement officer.

Signature

As applicable, sign and date *IN THE PRESENCE OF* a law enforcement officer, a notary, or a witness.

(21)   I certify that, to the best of my knowledge and belief, all of the information on and attached to this complaint is true, correct, and complete and made in good faith. I understand that this complaint or the information it contains may be made available to federal, state, and/or local law enforcement agencies for such action within their jurisdiction as they deem appropriate. I understand that knowingly making any false or fraudulent statement or representation to the government may violate federal, state, or local criminal statutes, and may result in a fine, imprisonment, or both.

_____   _____
Signature   Date Signed (mm/dd/yyyy)

Your Affidavit

(22)   If you do not choose to file a report with law enforcement, you may use this form as an Identity Theft Affidavit to prove to each of the companies where the thief misused your information that you are not responsible for the fraud. While many companies accept this affidavit, others require that you submit different forms. Check with each company to see if it accepts this form. You should also check to see if it requires notarization. If so, sign in the presence of a notary. If it does not, please have one witness (non-relative) sign that you completed and signed this Affidavit.

_____
Notary

Witness:

_____   _____
Signature   Printed Name

_____   _____
Date   Telephone Number

UNIFORM MINOR'S STATUS DECLARATION

This is a voluntary declaration for establishing that a child is a minor. Use it for disputes with credit reporting companies and creditors about identity theft related problems.

ABOUT THE MINOR CHILD

Full Legal Name
_____
First   Middle   Last, Suffix

Date of Birth _____   Social Security Number _____
mm/dd/yy

Current Street Address _____
City   State   Zip Code

The child has lived at
this address since _____
mm/dd/yy

All other addresses where the child has lived within the last five years:

_____

_____

_____

ABOUT THE PARENT, GUARDIAN, OR LEGAL REPRESENTATIVE

Full Legal Name
_____
First   Middle   Last, Suffix

Date of Birth _____
mm/dd/yy

Current Street Address
if different from the
child's address _____
City   State   Zip Code

I have lived at this
address since _____
mm/dd/yy

Daytime Telephone ( )_____   Evening Telephone ( )_____

DOCUMENTATION AND SIGNATURE

Attach COPIES, not originals, of the following documents with your Declaration:

- the child's birth certificate or, for an adopted child without a birth certificate, a final adoption proceeding order or certificate

- the child's Social Security card

- your state identification card, like a driver's license or military issued photo identification card that shows your current address

- a utility bill that shows your current address

- for guardians: a copy of the court order or another proof of guardianship or legal representation of the minor.

Sign and date the following paragraph:

I certify that, to the best of my knowledge and belief, all the information on and attached to this declaration is true, correct, and complete and made in good faith. I further certify that I am the parent, adoptive parent, legal guardian, or legal representative of the child named in this declaration. I understand that this declaration or the information it contains may be made available to federal, state, and/or local law enforcement agencies for such action within their jurisdiction as they deem appropriate. I understand that knowingly making a false or fraudulent statement or representation to the government may constitute a violation of 18 U.S.C. § 1001 or other federal, state, or local criminal statutes, and may result in imposition of a fine or imprisonment or both.

_____   _____
Signature   Date Signed

CONTACT INFO

CREDIT REPORTING COMPANIES

Equifax

www.equifax.com
1-800-525-6285

Experian

www.experian.com
1-888-397-3742

TransUnion

www.transunion.com
1-800-680-7289

Ask each company for the email or postal mail address for sending dispute or blocking requests.

FEDERAL GOVERNMENT

Federal Communications Commission

For help with telephone service:
www.fcc.gov/cgb

1-888-225-5322
1-888-835-5322 (TTY)

Federal Financial Institutions Examination Council

To locate the agency that regulates a bank or credit union:
www.ffiec.gov/consumercenter

Federal Trade Commission

To report identity theft:
www.ftc.gov/complaint

1-877-438-4338
1-866-653-4261 (TTY)

Internal Revenue Service

Identity Protection Specialized Unit

To report identity theft:
www.irs.gov/identitytheft

1-800-908-4490

Legal Services Programs

To locate a legal services provider:
www.lsc.gov/local-programs/program-profiles

Social Security Administration

To report fraud:
go to www.socialsecurity.gov and type "Fraud" in the Search box.

1-800-269-0271
1-866-501-2101 (TTY)

U.S. Department of Education

To report fraud:
www.ed.gov/about/offices/list/oig/hotline.html

Or go to www.ed.gov and type "OIG Hotline" in the Search box.

1-800-647-8733

U.S. Department of Justice

To report suspected bankruptcy fraud:
www.justice.gov/ust/eo/fraud

Or send email to
USTP.Bankruptcy.Fraud@usdoj.gov

U.S. Postal Inspection Service

To file a complaint:
https://postalinspectors.uspis.gov/contactUs/filecomplaint.aspx

1-877-876-2455

U.S. Postal Service

To place a hold on mail:
www.usps.com/holdmail

To locate a post office:
www.usps.com

1-800-275-8777

U.S. Securities and Exchange Commission

To report fraud:
www.sec.gov/complaint/tipscomplaint.shtml

1-800-732-0330

U.S. Department of State

To report a lost or stolen passport:
www.travel.state.gov/passport

1-877-487-2778
1-888-874-7793 (TDD/TTY)

OTHER

American Bar Association

To locate state and local bar associations:
www.americanbar.org/groups/bar_services/
resources/state_local_bar_associations.html

Certegy

To ask about a declined check:
www.askcertegy.com

1-800-437-5120

National Association of Attorneys General

To find a State Attorney General:
www.naag.org

1-202-326-6000 *(Not a toll-free number)*

Opt Out

To opt out of prescreened offers of credit or
insurance:
www.optoutprescreen.com

1-888-567-8688

Free Annual Credit Reports

To order a free annual credit report:
www.annualcreditreport.com

1-877-322-8228

ChexSystems, Inc.

To report checking accounts opened in
your name:
www.consumerdebit.com

1-800-428-9623

National Association of Regulatory Utility Commissioners

To get contact information for a state utility
commission:
www.naruc.org/commissions

1-202-898-2200 *(Not a toll-free number)*

TeleCheck Services, Inc.

To report check fraud:
www.firstdata.com/telecheck

1-800-710-9898